Birth and Early Years of Gandhiji's Life

Mahatma Gandhi is one of the most revered names in Indian history. He was the political and ideological leader of India, also honoured as Father of our nation, he became an international symbol of the free India. He played a very important role in the Indian freedom movement. He is lovingly called as Bapu. His teachings of 'Ahinsa' and 'Satya' (non-violence and truth) changed the complete outlook of the Indian freedom fighters.

Mohan Das Karamchand Gandhi, also known as Mahatma Gandhi, was born on 2nd October 1869 in a Hindu family of Porbandar, Gujarat. His parents were Karamchand Gandhi and Putlibai.

His father, Karamchand Gandhi was a Diwan (Chief Minister) of Porbandar and an honourable and upright man. Gandhiji's mother was a religious and pious woman. Gandhiji gained high moral and social values from his parents. Since childhood, Gandhiji believed strongly in non-violence, truth, purity and very simple lifestyle.

At the age of 13, Gandhiji got married to a girl of the same age named, Kasturba Gandhi. They had four sons. Gandhiji started his education in Porbandar. He further studied in Rajkot and did his matriculation. Then, he joined the University of Bombay in 1887. His family wanted him to become a barrister.

In 1888, he went to London for further studies and completed his law in 1891. He returned to India. For the next two years, he practised law in India.

Gandhiji in South Africa

At the age of 23, Gandhiji left his family once again and came to South Africa as a legal advisor of an Indian businessman. In South Africa, Gandhiji found that there was a strong demarcation between the Black and White communities. The Black community faced a lot of discrimination and were very badly treated. Gandhiji felt very bad about this.

Just after a week of his stay, Gandhiji experienced the humiliation because of discrimination. One day, he had to travel in a train. He had a first-class ticket with him. At the Pietermartizburg station when he entered the first-class compartment and was asked to shift to the third-class compartment. The ticket checker told him that the first-class was reserved for Whites.

On raising objection on this discrimination, Gandhiji was thrown out of the train.

During this journey, he late came to know that discrimination is the common practise there. The Black community and the Indians were called 'coolies'.

After this incident, Gandhiji decided to fight against this injustice. He wrote letters to the higher officials and began a protest against the discrimination in South Africa.

For the next three years, Gandhiji continuously fought for the justice. Soon, he became a well-known activist and a leader of the Indian community.

On 22nd May 1894, Gandhiji established an organisation—Natal Indian Congress (NIC) in South Africa. This organisation looked after the rights of Indians living there. While working for NIC, Gandhiji also faced a lot of opposition from the other communities. He was also attacked several times.

Gandhiji spent twenty years in South Africa. Thereafter, in the year 1915, he returned to India.

Gandhiji in India

Gandhiji's struggles and successes in South Africa were well known in India also. He became a 'National Hero' in the eyes of Indians. Gandhiji wanted to create the same wave of reformation in India. He travelled to all the parts of India to know the real conditions of Indians.

While his travels, Gandhiji used to wear a dhoti and wooden slippers. He renounced all the pleasures and adopted a very simple lifestyle.

He established the 'Sabarmati Ashram' in Ahmedabad, Gujarat. He lived in the ashram with his family and some of his supporters. Everyone loved and supported Gandhiji.

People started believing in his teachings of non-violence and truth. He got the title of 'Mahatma', which meant 'a great soul'.

The Indian Freedom Movement

India was under British rule at that time. A large number of freedom fighters were fighting for the freedom of India. Gandhiji also wanted the freedom of India but he followed a different path. He began a non-violent movement called 'Satyagraha' against the British.

Satyagraha means opposition, but not in an aggressive form. Gandhiji taught people to ask for justice in a silent way. The movement created a strong wave and became a great success.

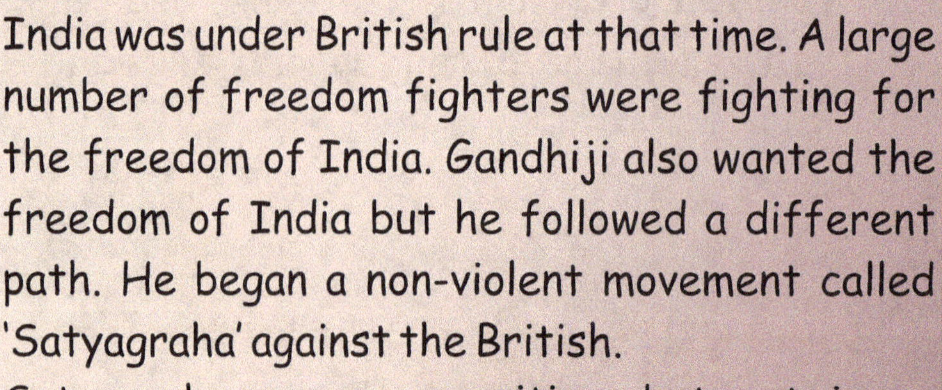

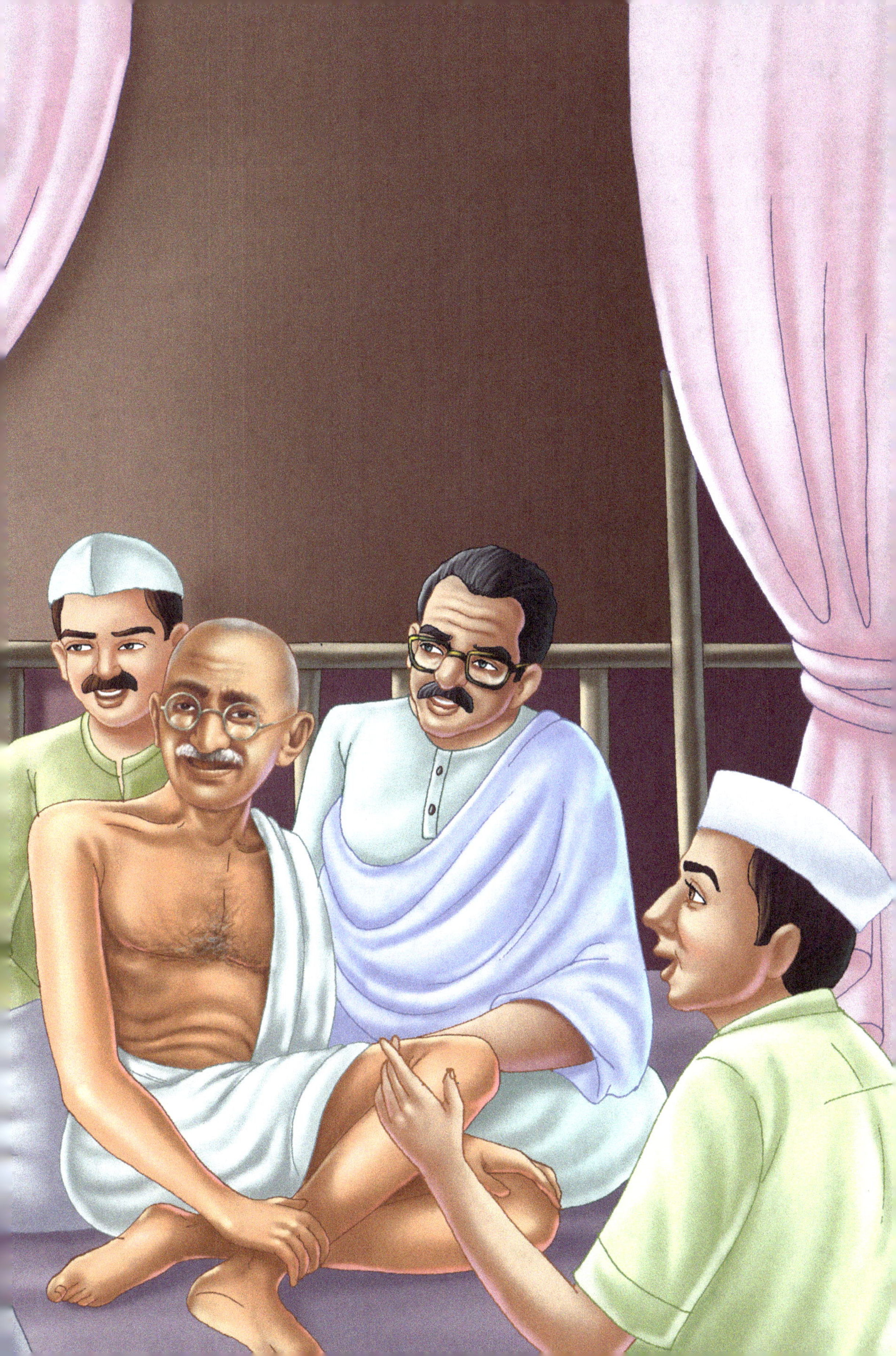

In 1919-20, Gandhiji started another movement called 'Non-cooperative movement'. During his struggle for freedom, Gandhiji was sent to jail many times by the British Govt, but he continued his mission. He asked indians to stop using foreign clothes and other things. He insisted to spin natural cloth on Charkha (spinning wheel). The image of the Charkha later became a symbol of the Indian independence.

On 12th March 1930, Gandhi ji began 'Dandi March' or the 'Salt March' against the salt tax. Gandhi ji with his supporters stand walking 200 miles from Sabarmati Ashram towards the sea.

On April 5, the group reached Dandi, a place along the Coast. Gandhiji demonstrated the method to make salt from the seawater. Soon, the movement spread in the entire nation. Gandhiji was imprisoned once again but, the protest continued nationwide. It was stopped only after the 'Delhi Pact' between the British Government and Gandhiji. The Pact granted the limited salt production and all the protestors were released.

In 1942, Gandhiji issued the last call for independence from British rule. He initiated another movement called 'August Kranti.' Soon after, he began 'Quit India' movement that asked the Britishers to leave India.

After the long struggle and sacrifices, India became independent on 15th August 1947. At the time of freedom, India faced the partition in two parts. After the freedom, Gandhiji tried to maintain peace and unity among the people of different communities.

There was a lot of disturbance in all the parts of country. The communal violence was spreading fast. To stop this violence, Gandhiji began a 'fast unto death' on 13th January 1948 which proved to be a success. On 18th January 1948, he ended his fast only when he got the assurance that the communal violence would be stopped.

Assassination of Gandhiji

Some Indians believed that Gandhiji was responsible for the partition of India. Gandhiji faced a lot of opposition. On the unfortunate day of 30th January 1948, Gandhiji was going to address a prayer meeting. He was walking along with his two assistants—Abha and Manu. Just when he was stepping towards the stage to address the public, a man named Nathuram Godse fired at Gandhiji. Gandhiji fell on the ground, saying, "Hey Ram, Hey Ram!" These were the last words of Mahatma Gandhi.

The great soul, the light of the nation, was gone. The whole country was mourning bitterly on their dear Bapu's departure from the world. The other countries were also shocked at his death.

Soon after the assassination of Mahatma Gandhi, Pt. Jawahar Lal Nehru addressed the nation on radio:

"Friends & Comarades, The light has gone out of our lives and there is darkness everywhere. I do not know what to tell you and how to say it. Our beloved leader, Bapu as we called him, the Father of the Nation, is no more.

Perhaps I am wrong to say that. Nevertheless, we will never see him again as we have seen him for these many years. We will not run to him for advice and seek solace from him, and that is a terrible blow, not only to me, but also to millions and millions in this country.

And it is a little difficult to soften the blow by any other advice that I or anyone else can give you.."

India Remembers Mahatma Gandhi

Mahatma Gandhi's Samadhi is at Raj Ghat in Delhi. Thousands of people from all over the country come to Raj Ghat to pay homage to the great man.

2nd October, Gandhiji's birthday is celebrated as 'Gandhi Jayanti'. It is one of the three National festivals of India. People of India still remember their dear 'Bapu' with great love and reverence.

Every year, 30th January—the day of Gandhiji's assassination, is observed as the Martyr's Day to commemorate the struggle of all those who sacrificed their life for the country. Mahatma Gandhi's picture is also printed on the Indian currency notes.

Mahatma Gandhi was a great writer also. He wrote and edited many newspaper articles during his lifetime. He also wrote several books including his autobiography—My Experiments with Truth.

In the year 1930, Time magazine named Mahatma Gandhi as 'The Man of the Year'. There are many books written about him and his teachings. The life of Mahatma Gandhi has been widely portrayed in the Indian literature, theatre and movies.

Mahatma Gandhi dedicated his entire life for the welfare of Indians. He has been the greatest source of inspiration for all the Indians. His teachings of non-violence, peace and truth are still practised and followed by many, not only in India but also in other countries.

The only way to pay tribute to the great man—The Father of Our Nation—is to follow his teachings in our lives. We should learn from the great life of Mahatma Gandhi.

Birth and Early Years of Mother Teresa

Mother Teresa is one of the most revered names in the World. She was a Roman Catholic nun of Albanian ethnicity and Indian citizenship. She dedicated her entire life in serving the poor and needy. She has been a source of inspiration for the human kind. Her real name was Agnes Gonxha Bojaxhiu.

Agnes was born on 26th August 1910 in the city of Skopje (now capital of Republic of Macedonia) in Yugoslavia. But she considered 27th August as her birthday when she was baptized. She was the youngest of three children to an Albanian Catholic couple—Nikola and Dranafile Bojaxhiu. Nikola was a self-made successful businessman.

In 1919, when Agnes was just nine-years old, her father suddenly died. It was a very difficult time for Agnes' mother. But she faced the circumstances and began a new life to fulfil the responsibility of her three children. She started selling textiles and hand-made embroidery. She gave good moral values to her kids. Agnes and her sisters were very religious and used to pray every day.

Since childhood, Agnes was fascinated by the lives of Missionaries. She had a pure and kind heart. One day, Agnes and her sisters were playing with some poor street children. Their mother saw them and became very upset. She called them inside and said, "Don't play with such dirty and uncultured kids! Do you want to become like them?"

Agnes' sisters remained silent. But Agnes replied, "Dear Mother, why do we think of avoiding these kids? Can't we change them and make them like us? You always teach us to help the poor and needy. Then, why are you stopping us today to play with them?"

Agnes' mother was touched to hear her words. She said, "My dear, you're absolutely correct. We should not avoid such children. We should rather try to change their lives by giving them love and support."

When Agnes was just twelve-years old, she became more considerate towards humankind. She started thinking to become a nun to serve humanity. She knew that becoming a nun was not easy. She also knew that a nun could not marry and have her own family. She would have to leave everything behind. She thought more seriously before taking this decision.

Agnes regularly accompanied her mother to the church and performed charity programmes.

Agnes had heard a lot about the Catholic Missionaries working in India. She applied to the Loreto order of Nuns based in Ireland but had missions in India.

Agnes Becomes a Nun

In September 1928, Agnes left her home at the age of eighteen to join Loreto, Ireland as a missionary. She spent six weeks in Ireland, studied about the history of Loreto and took special training in English language to teach the school children in India.

In 1929, Agnes arrived in India. It took her more than two years to become a nun. Finally, on 24th May 1931, she took her first vow as a nun of Loreto. As a Loreto nun, she chose a new name for herself based on Saint Teresa. Since then, she was called as Sister Teresa. She joined Loreto Convent in Kolkata (known as Calcutta earlier) and started teaching the school children.

Mother Teresa was highly moved to see the conditions of poor people in India who didn't even have the basic necessities like food, clothes and homes.

Mother Teresa's heart was filled with sympathy for the poor. She could feel their pain and agony. She also renounced her fine dress of Loreto and wore a simple dress made of very thin fabric.

Loreto nuns were usually not allowed to teach outside the premises of the convent. But a special exemption was given to Mother Teresa to teach outside the St. Teresa's Convent.

After spending two years there, she took her final vow in
May 1937. She, then, officially became Mother Teresa.
She became the Headmistress of St. Mary's Convent and
served there for twenty years. But she was also highly
concerned about the poor and needy.

The Bengal famine in 1943 brought misery, diseases and deaths in the city. Then, the violence during the Hindu-Muslim riots in August 1946 further worsened the conditions.

Being Indian at heart, mother Teresa in 1948 adopted Indian citizenship and decided to start a Missionary of Charity. She had to select a dress for the Missionary. She chose a white saree with blue border as her official dress. This was the dress worn by the Municipal women sweepers at that time.

Mother Teresa took the dress to the Church. She requested the Father to bless the dress. Father at the church looked at her and said, "Do you know, this is the dress worn by the sweepers? And, they're considered as untouchables."

"Father, this is the reason I chose this dress. I want to be identified with the poorest and the lowest of the land. My mission is to eradicate their poverty and diseases. I want to share their pain and agony," replied Mother Teresa.

Father's eyes were filled with tears. He blessed the dress and prayed to the God to grant success to Mother Teresa's mission.

Great Works of Mother Teresa

Mother Teresa began the preparations for starting the Missionary of Charities. She led a simple life and lived in a small room. Her only possessions were a small wooden box and a framed picture of Mother Mary.

The mission of her organisation was to accept the poor people with open arms and love them. She opened a school for slum children at Moti Jheel. The children who studied in her school became extremely well mannered and cultured.

Slowly and gradually, the school flourished and it got shifted from an open area to a two-room house. One room was used as a clinic to attend the sick people. More and more volunteers joined and supported Mother Teresa's mission. She approached the poor people to understand their problems and tried her best to solve them. Her great work started getting recognition and praise from everywhere.

On 15th August 1947, India became independent. In December 1947, Mother Teresa organised a Christmas celebration in a government school. The Chief Minister of West Bengal was the Chief Guest of the occasion.

The Prime Minister of India, Pt. Jawahar Lal Nehru, happened to be in Kolkata at that time. He sent a message to Mother Teresa that he too wanted to attend the function.

Mother Teresa sent a reply that it would be a great privilege for her and the organisation to have him as a guest.

Pt. Jawahar Lal Nehru attended the function and praised Mother Teresa's efforts. He also promised to help the organisation in all the possible ways.

In 1950, a woman was left outside Mother Teresa's Home by her sons. She was suffering from leprosy, so her sons abandoned her. Mother Teresa realised that there were many people suffering from this disease. Their families used to leave them on roadsides because of their disease. Mother Teresa then started a Home for Lepers in Teetagarh with the help of other sister of her organisation. She gave shelter and medication to many lepers.

Mother Teresa then opened many homes to give shelter to the poor and needy. 'Nirmal Hriday' was one of these houses for sick near Kalighat temple in Kolkata. With the support of authorities and volunteers, the number of Mother homes were growing day by day in many cities of India. With the insistence of Pope John Paul II, Mother Teresa opened the first overseas home in Venezuela.

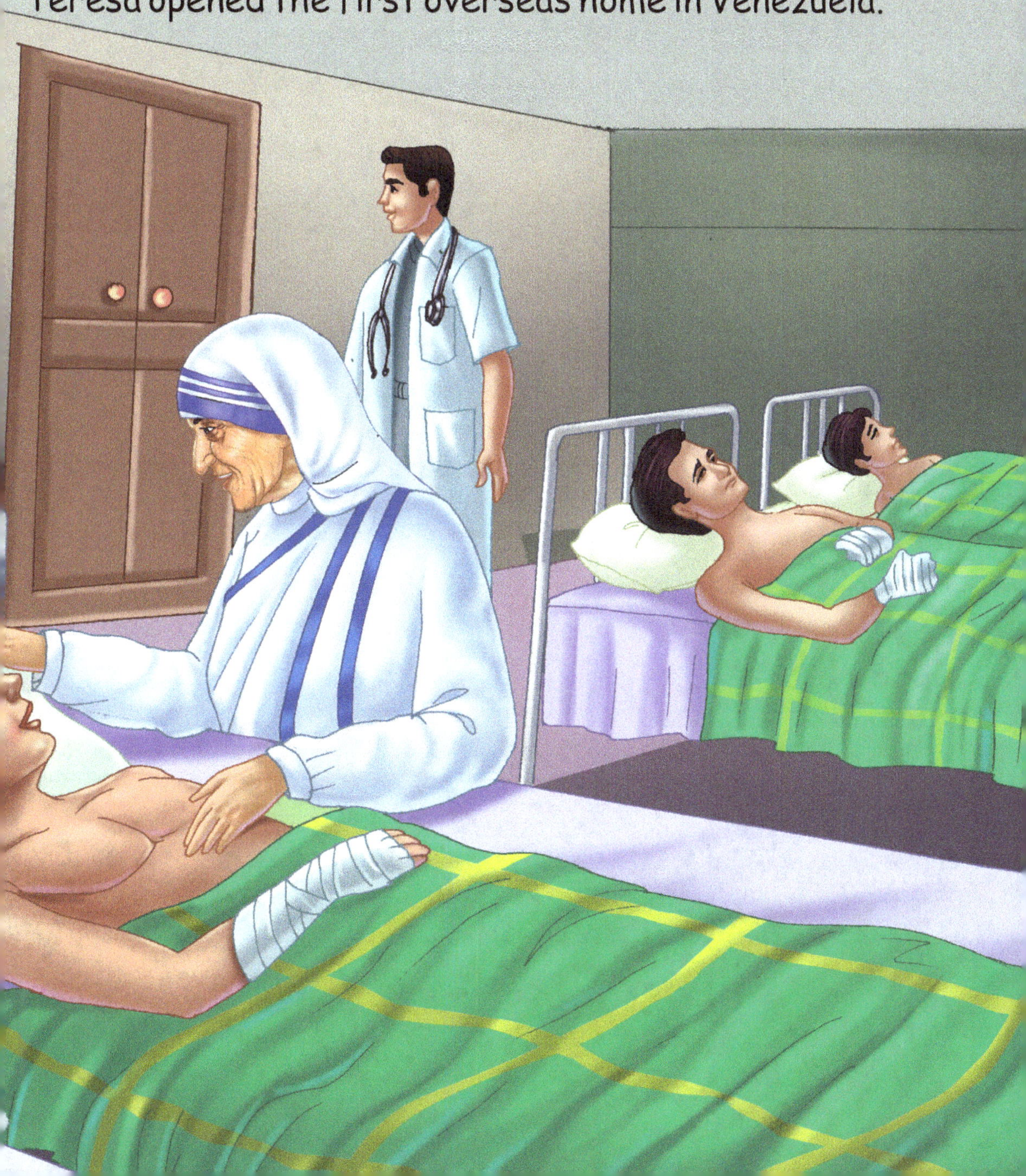

Mother Teresa and the sisters also visited many war zones and cured the injured and sick people. With the support of many people, she started orphanages, old age homes, schools, hospitals etc. to serve people.

Mother Teresa and her mission became well known everywhere. She received many rewards and many honours.

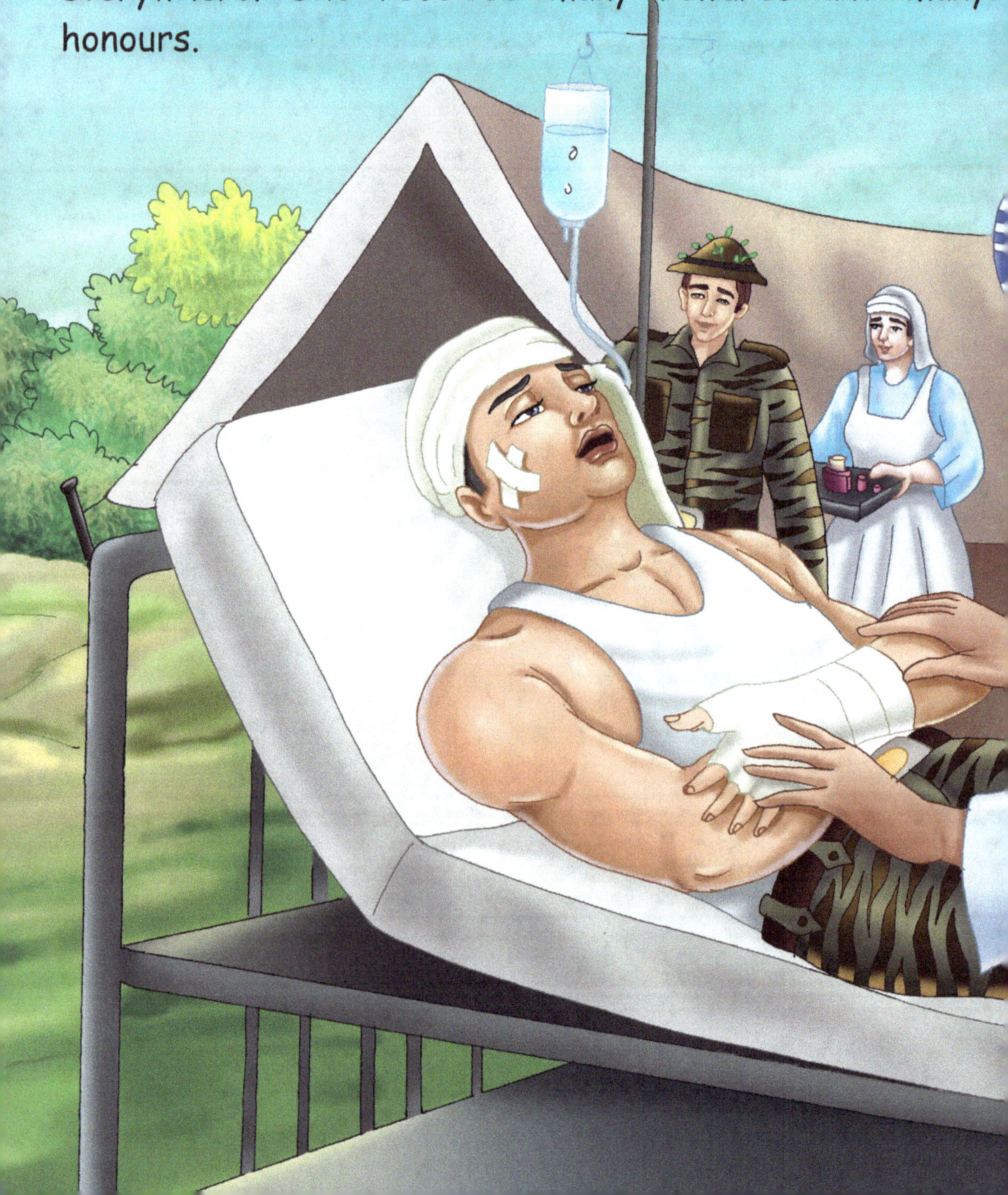

In 1979, she received Noble Prize for her exceptional work in social welfare.
Apart from this, she got more than 50 national and international awards for her work. She was honoured in India and abroad by various awards like Bharat Ratna, The Leo Tolstoy Award, The Magasaysay Award, The Peace Prize, The Kennedy Award and many more.

The Last Phase of Mother Teresa's Life

In 1983, Mother Teresa suffered a heart attack followed by another in 1989. She offered to resign as the head of missionaries of charity, but nuns in a secret ballot voted for her to stay. With a gradual health decline, she finally resigned from the post in March 1997. She died on 5th september 1997.

The whole world mourned on her death. Mother Teresa was a living legend. It was the biggest loss to our humanity. She brought the message of love, humility and compassion. There are thousands of stories about her greatness. Her selfless work, sacrifice, dedication, love and kindness will always remain memorable. We should all learn and draw inspiration from her life.